Savvy

Girls Rock

W0006766

MW010 38 09 b

GIRLS RACE!

AMAZING TALES OF WOMEN IN SPORTS

BY KATHY ALLEN

Consultant: Yolanda L. Jackson
Senior Director, Athlete Services
Women's Sports Foundation
New York, New York

CAPSTONE PRESS
a capstone imprint

Savvy Books are published by Capstone Press,
1710 Roe Crest Drive, North Mankato, Minnesota 56003
www.capstonepub.com

Library of Congress Cataloging-in-Publication Data
Allen, Kathy.
Girls race! : amazing tales of women in sports / by Kathy Allen.
pages cm.—(Savvy. Girls rock!)
Includes bibliographical references and index.
Summary: "Through narrative stories, explores female athletes who have made major contributions to sports and culture"—Provided by publisher.
ISBN 978-1-4765-0233-5 (library binding) — ISBN 978-1-4765-3563-0 (ebook pdf)
1. Women athletes—Biography—Juvenile literature. I. Title.
 GV697.A1A437 2014
 796.092'52—dc23
 [B]   2012051153

Editorial Credits
Jennifer Besel, editor; Veronica Scott, designer; Svetlana Zhurkin, media researcher; Laura Manthe, production specialist

Photo Credits
AP Photo: Ron Edmonds, 45, Str, 6; Corbis: Bettmann, 8, 15 (top), 21 (top), 27, 60 (bottom left), Colorsport, 31 (top), Demotix/R. Jeanette Martin, 14 (bottom), Duomo, 49, Jerry Cooke, 20 (bottom), Steve Boyle, 21 (bottom), TempSport/Gilbert Iundt, 43 (top); Getty Images: Allsport/Tony Duffy, 4–5, Phil Cole, 33, Popperfoto, 12; Library of Congress, 11, 34 (right), 37 (top), 57; Newscom: AFP/George Frey, 32, AFP/Jeff Haynes, 61 (bottom right), AFP/Timothy Clary, 9 (top), Icon SMI/Imago/Werek, 61 (bottom left), Icon SMI/Jeffrey Corder, 21 (middle), Mirrorpix, 13, Picture History/Ira L. Hills, 56, Popperfoto/united archives/kpa, 17, 46 (bottom), Roll Call/Tom Williams, 34 (left), sportfotodienst/Imago, 39, SportsChrome/Andrew Gombert, 53, SportsChrome/Michael Zito, 42 (bottom), SportsChrome/Sport The Library, 29, united archives/kpa, 40–41, UPI Photo Service/Monika Graff, 25, UPI Photo Service/Tsar Fedorsky, 37 (bottom), ZUMA Press/Bay Area News Group, 51, ZUMA Press/Bruce Stotesbury, 20 (top), ZUMA Press/Keystone Pictures USA, 46 (top), ZUMA Press/Martin Philbey, 22, ZUMA Press/Sacramento Bee, 19; Shutterstock: Anna Paff, 35, baldyrgan, 14 (top), Beelde Photography, 43 (bottom), Chris Mole, 15 (bottom), file404, 64, FlashStudio, 55, gudinny, 23 (back), hugolacasse, 58 (top), 59 (top), Jarvis Gray, 30, Leremy, 44, Lev Radin, 54, Mai Techaphan, 58 (bottom), Natalie Jean, 47, ODM Studio, 60–61 (back), Ozger Aybike Sarikaya, cover, back cover, 1, paintings, 30–31 (back), 32–33 (back), Pete Saloutos, 3, Phil Anthony, 60 (bottom right), Photo Works, 9 (bottom), photogolfer, 59 (bottom), Sandra Matic, 8–9 (back), Sarunyu_foto, 52, Suti Gallery, 54–55 (back), Val Lawless, 58–59 (back), Valentin Agapov, 16–17 (back), Valik-Novik, 7, Vectomart, 62, VikaSuh, 56–57 (back), Warren Price Photography, 31 (bottom), Webitect, 42 (top), Zhu Difeng, 50–51 (back), zippy, 50; University of Massachusetts Amherst: W.E.B. Du Bois Library/Department of Special Collections and University Archives, 36

Direct quotations are placed within quotation marks and appear on the following pages. Other pieces written in first-person point of view are works of creative nonfiction by the author.
p3: http://www.biography.com/people/billie-jean-king-9364876; p11: *How to Be Like Women Athletes of Influence: 32 Women at the Top of Their Game and How You Can Get There Too* by Pat Williams and Dana Pennett O'Neil (Deerfield Beach, Fla.: Health Communications, Inc., 2007); p12: http://espn.go.com/classic/biography/s/King_Billie_Jean.html; p13: http://sports.espn.go.com/sports/tennis/usopen06/news/story?id=2578105; p19: http://www.oandp.com/facilities/pa/carter/newsletter.htm; p20: http://espn.go.com/abcsports/s/2001/0417/1174371.html; p23: http://www.vice.com/epicly-later-d/elissa-steamer-part-1; http://www.vice.com/epicly-later-d/elissa-steamer-part-4; p47: http://www.sidewalkstv.com/webclips/r/marylouretton.html; p50: http://articles.washingtonpost.com/2012-08-08/sports/35493745_1_walsh-jennings-americans-april-ross-jennifer-kessy; p53: *Go for the Gold: A Champion's Guide to Winning Soccer and Life* by Mia Hamm (New York: Quill, 2000); p57: http://www.nytimes.com/video/2012/02/08/sports/100000001322750/dancer-as-athlete.html; p59: http://sports.espn.go.com/espn/espn25/story?page=moments/44; p62: *The Olympic Odyssey: Rekindling the True Spirit of the Great Games* by Phil Cousineau (Wheaton, Ill.: Quest Books, 2003)

Printed in the United States of America in Stevens Point, Wisconsin.
032013   007227WZF13

PLAY LIKE A GIRL

THEY WERE TOLD THEY COULDN'T COMPETE.

THEY WERE TOLD THEY WOULD EMBARRASS THE SPORT.

THEY WERE TOLD THEY WERE "JUST GIRLS."

Female athletes not only fought for every ribbon and trophy they earned, they fought against every limit placed upon them. They
pushed farther,
soared faster,
held firmer
to beat even their own expectations.

The women in this book broke barriers, set world records, and changed the world of sports forever. Female athletes have overcome obstacles and beat the odds with grace and skill. Along the way they've inspired countless young women to stand tall and play like a girl.

"A CHAMPION IS AFRAID OF LOSING. EVERYONE ELSE IS AFRAID OF WINNING."

– BILLIE JEAN KING

JACKIE JOYNER-KERSEE

MARCH 3, 1962–

In her first track race, Jackie Joyner-Kersee came in dead last. But she was just 9 years old. And she didn't quit. In fact, it made her strive to get better.

In high school Joyner-Kersee became a track and field star. She set the record in her school for the best long jump at 20 feet, 7½ inches (6.3 meters). By the time she came to the 1986 Goodwill Games in Moscow, Russia, she was one of the world's best in track and field. Her event was the heptathlon.

Those games turned out to be history-making. Joyner-Kersee blew the competition away. When the dust had settled, she had scored 7,148 points—a new world record.

Before she retired Joyner-Kersee earned more than 7,000 points in heptathlon competitions six times. She won gold at the 1988 and 1992 Olympics. And she had made and broken her own world records, becoming one of the greatest track and field athletes of all time.

HEPTATHLON

MADE UP OF SEVEN CONTESTS, THE HEPTATHLON IS SPREAD OVER TWO DAYS.

- 100-M HURDLES
- HIGH JUMP
- SHOT PUT
- 200-M RUN
- LONG JUMP
- JAVELIN THROW
- 800-M RUN

ANN TRASON

AUGUST 30, 1960–

know every turn and twist of these trails. keep my gaze steady ahead, anticipating what each rock or twist in the trail might bring. I have been running for 17 hours.

When I began the race, I was running with a group of 246 die-hard trail runners. Now, I run alone. Most of them are behind me, although it is hard to keep track of other runners. I have climbed through forests and snow cover. I've waded through waist-high water in the low canyons. I must try to focus and think clearly. I cannot miss the trail markers that will guide me to the finish.

As I run I think back to the first two times I entered this race. Both times I had to drop out. I have come so far since then, I can't stop now. I listen for the cheers, whistles, and cowbells that will greet me at the finish. At times I think I hear them, but it could be my mind playing tricks on me. Above all else, I must keep running.

Ann Trason is an ultramarathon legend. She runs races that are up to 100 miles (161 kilometers) long. But she's not a legend just because of the distances she runs. She's a legend because she runs them so fast. She holds a course record for the Western States race, a 100-mile (161-km) trek. She ran that distance in just 17 hours, 37 minutes

This running superstar has broken 20 world records, won the Western States 14 times

... and leaves everyone awed by her power.

COMPARING LONG-DISTANCE RACES:

WESTERN STATES: 100 MILES (161 KM)

WORLD 100K CHALLENGE: 62 MILES (100 KM)

COMRADES MARATHON: 56 MILES (90 KM)

MARATHON: 26.2 MILES (42 KM)

HOOPS STARS

There was a time when there was no such thing as a professional women's basketball player. That changed with the creation of the Women's National Basketball Association (WNBA) in 1996. Before the WNBA college hoops stars like Cheryl Miller helped popularize the sport. WNBA powerhouses like Sheryl Swoopes and Lisa Leslie proved that the women in basketball were just as tough and talented as the men.

CHERYL MILLER

JANUARY 3, 1964–

Before the WNBA female basketball players made a name for themselves on the college circuit, and Cheryl Miller was one of the best. Miller played the forward position for the University of Southern California. In four years, she led her team to 112 wins and just 20 losses. She earned All-American honors in each of her four seasons and was a three-time NCAA player of the year. In 1984 Miller also led the U.S. Olympic team to a gold medal.

CAREER STATS	
3,018 points	1,534 rebounds

SHERYL SWOOPES

MARCH 25, 1971–

The sport of women's basketball was ready for prime time when the WNBA was created in 1996. The first famous face of the association was Sheryl Swoopes. The college standout was the first player signed to a WNBA team, the Houston Comets. In her career with the Comets, Swoopes was a four-time WNBA champion and three-time WNBA most valuable player. She also won three Olympic gold medals with the U.S. Olympic team.

CAREER STATS

4,875 points	1,037 assists
1,596 rebounds	657 steals

LISA LESLIE

JULY 7, 1972–

The seventh player to be signed in that first WNBA draft was Lisa Leslie. Leslie came from a successful high school and college basketball career. In college she set records at the University of Southern California for scoring, blocking, and rebounding. In her career in the WNBA, she became the first player to score 6,000 points. She was also the first player in the WNBA to dunk the ball. Leslie was a three-time WNBA most valuable player. She also won four Olympic gold medals with the U.S. Olympic team.

CAREER STATS

6,263 points	874 assists
3,307 rebounds	492 steals

BABE DIDRIKSON ZAHARIAS

JUNE 26, 1911—SEPTEMBER 27, 1956

As teams gathered at the 1932 National Women's AAU Track Meet, Babe Didrikson Zaharias showed up alone. Zaharias was the star player on a basketball team organized by the Employer Casualty Company. The company saw what a great all-around athlete Zaharias was, so it sent her to the 1932 track meet. She didn't have a team, but she was ready to compete.

IN THREE HOURS ZAHARIAS WON FIVE EVENTS:

80-M HURDLES	JAVELIN
BROAD JUMP	SHOT PUT
BASEBALL THROW	

She not only beat every other athlete, she earned more points than any team of athletes. The second place team, with 22 athletes, trailed her by eight points. "Team Babe" won the meet single-handedly.

No sport was beyond Zaharias' reach. She played golf, tennis, basketball, cycling, swimming, and diving, to name a few. With her muscles, grit, and confidence, she competed unlike any athlete the world had seen. Today she is considered one of the greatest athletes of all time.

1932

She qualifies for five Olympic events. Women are allowed to compete in only three. Zaharias
- wins the women's Olympic javelin.
- wins the 80-m hurdles and sets a world record.
- breaks the world record in high-jump, but is awarded the silver medal due to a judging decision

1933

Zaharias begins competing in golf tournaments.

1935

After winning the Texas Women's Amateur golf tournament, officials rule Zaharias is not an amateur because she has competed professionally in other sports.

1935 TO 1943

Zaharias continues to golf. But she also plays as many as 17 sets of tennis each

ZAHARIAS WAS ONCE ASKED IF THERE WAS ANYTHING SHE DIDN'T PLAY. SHE REPLIED, "YEAH, DOLLS."

1943 — 1945 — 1947 — 1948 — 1950

1943 — She is reinstated as a golf amateur and begins competing again.

1945 — Zaharias is named Female Athlete of the Year by the Associated Press; she would win that honor a total of six times.

1947 — Zaharias turns golf pro and wins 17 out of 18 tournaments.

1948 — Zaharias wins the U.S. Women's Open, the World Championship, and the All-American Open as a pro golfer.

1950 — Zaharias is named Greatest Female Athlete of the first half of the 20th

BILLIE JEAN KING

NOVEMBER 22, 1943–

It was definitely a different time back then. The '70s were a time when U.S. women had to stand up for equal rights. At work women fought for better jobs and equal pay. At home we fought for respect and independence. In sports we fought to be recognized as powerful athletes. It wasn't easy. Many men, like tennis star Bobby Riggs, made it clear they thought they were better than women.

Riggs boasted that he could beat any woman on the tennis court. There's no doubt he was a great player. But there's no doubt he had a big ego too. I agreed to play Riggs.

They say 50 million people tuned into our tennis match September 20, 1973. "The Battle of the Sexes" they called it. I worried that losing would destroy the work women had done to be treated equally.

That match was the most intense of my life. I couldn't let Riggs win. I didn't let him win. I won all three sets that day. It was a great day to be a woman.

"I thought it would set us back 50 years if I didn't win that match."

Between 1961 and 1979, Billie Jean King won 20 Wimbledon titles. She also won 13 U.S. titles, four French titles, and two Australian titles.

MARTINA NAVRATILOVA

OCTOBER 18, 1956–

When Billie Jean King was fighting "The Battle of the Sexes," I was a young tennis player just starting to make headlines. It's amazing, but King later called me the greatest tennis player who ever lived. I'm not sure about that. But I did pretty well.

In my career, I won a total of 59 Grand Slam titles. From 1982 to 1984, I lost only six matches. In 2003 I won the Wimbledon mixed doubles title at the age of 46 years, 261 days, becoming the oldest Wimbledon champion.

"Don't get limited by people that say, 'No, you can't do that because you're too old or because you're heavy or you're not an athlete.' Whatever your limitations might be, don't let them define you. I didn't let it define me."

GREAT RIVALS

Nothing makes a great athlete like a great rivalry. Navratilova's chief rival in the 1970s was Chris Evert. While Navratilova won more tournaments, Evert became the first player ever to win 1,000 singles matches.

Navratilova and Evert paved the way for another famous rivalry between Steffi Graf and Monica Seles. In 1998 Graf passed Navratilova as the highest-earning women's tennis player. Her rival, Seles, became the youngest player ever to be ranked number one. She was just 17.

KATHRINE SWITZER
JANUARY 5, 1947–

Kathrine Switzer entered the 1967 Boston marathon under the name "K." The race was not officially open to women, but that wasn't going to stop Switzer. Shortly after the run began, the race director tried to stop her and rip off her number. But Switzer just kept running. Twenty-six miles later, Switzer had proven to the world that a woman could run the distance. Her well-publicized run played a part in the Amateur Athletics Union's 1971 decision to allow female athletes to compete in marathons.

The sport of women's long-distance running has come a long way. In three decades women marathoners have shaved about 15 minutes off the time it takes to run the grueling 26.2 miles (42 km) of a marathon. A woman has yet to reach the men's record time of 2 hours, 3 minutes. But some powerful runners have blazed the trail toward making that once distant dream a reality.

GRETE WAITZ
OCTOBER 1, 1953–APRIL 19, 2011

The 1978 New York City marathon was the first marathon Grete Waitz ever ran. She was a competitive runner at shorter distances, but she had never run a marathon. Her finish shocked everyone. She not only won the race, but she set a world record doing it. The young, pig-tailed Waitz made it look easy. She had trained herself into a standout track athlete, setting world records in the 3,000-m, 8-km, 10-km, 15-km and 10-mile races. And she won the New York City Marathon nine times, more than any other runner.

PAULA RADCLIFFE
DECEMBER 17, 1973–

Like Grete Waitz, Paula Radcliffe began her running career with shorter distances. She holds world records in road races, including the 10- and 20-km races. But Radcliffe is best known as a marathoner. In her first competitive marathon, the 2002 London Marathon, she ran the 26.2 miles (42 km) in 2 hours, 18 minutes, 56 seconds. She later set a women's world record on the same course in 2:15:25. She still holds the women's marathon world record.

Sonja Henie

APRIL 8, 1912–OCTOBER 12, 1969

The darling of the figure skating world in the 1920s was young Sonja Henie. A graceful beauty from Norway, Henie was winning championships at just 10 years old. She revolutionized figure skating.

Henie merged her ballet training and her skills on the ice to create programs unlike anything done before. She was the first skater to skate to the music instead of just having music as background noise.

Here is her stellar career by the numbers.

6 Henie was just 6 years old when she began figure skating.

10 Henie won 10 world championships in a row.

80 Henie could complete a dizzying 80 revolutions while spinning on the ice.

3 She won three Olympic gold medals, the most of any female figure skater ever.

13 Henie also starred in 13 films, becoming a successful actress too.

STYLE SETTERS

When Henie began her career, it was not acceptable for women to wear short skirts—on the ice or off. They were expected to wear ankle-length skirts, which is not the best for skating. Henie had a different idea. She was the first figure skater to wear a skirt above the knee. Audiences loved her beautiful dresses, which were more like costumes than street clothes.

Another leg-bearing pioneer, Lili de Alvarez, was the first female tennis player to wear shorts, shaking up the tennis world at Wimbledon in 1931.

But neither Henie nor Alvarez faced the backlash that Annette Kellerman did nearly 25 years earlier. The champion swimmer was arrested on a beach for wearing a bathing suit that police called "indecent." The one-piece suit was sleeveless and had shorts that exposed her thighs.

AMY
PALMIERO-WINTERS

AUGUST 18, 1972–

In the dark of night, the pounding of feet keeps a steady beat. These runners have been going for hours. By the time they are done, they will have run for 24 straight hours and completed an amazing 130 miles (209 km).

This race—the Run to the Future race—is grueling. Just finishing is an honor. But to win it? Winning would earn a spot on the U.S. national track and field team.

As the sun rises, one runner stands out. A 37-year-old woman pushes herself to go faster. And when she crosses the finish line first, she makes history.

She didn't make history because she's a woman. Her age isn't record-breaking, either. Amy Palmiero-Winters is groundbreaking because of what she doesn't have. She is the first amputee to make the U.S. track team.

Palmiero-Winters lost her left leg after an accident when she was 22 years old. But she did not lose her determination and passion for running. Today she competes in marathons, triathlons, Ironman triathlons, and ultramarathons. And she does it all with a prosthetic running blade.

Palmiero-Winters' running blade is designed to help absorb the impact of running such long distances. A piece of car tire is attached to the foot to give it traction. But running with a prosthetic can be dangerous. During one summer race, the heat from the road rose through Palmiero-Winters' prosthetic. That heat caused third-degree burns on her limb.

"I WANT TO DO THIS FOR MY KIDS ... IT'S NOT ALL ABOUT ME,
IT'S ALSO FOR THEM. WHEN THEY GET OLDER, THEY'LL KNOW
WHAT I HAVE DONE, AND THAT THEY CAN SET GOALS, AND BE
ABLE TO REACH THEM. THE ONLY LIMITS THEY HAVE ARE THE
ONES THEY SET FOR THEMSELVES. LIFE IS WHAT YOU MAKE IT."

A WOMAN'S WORLD

Professional baseball, horse racing, race car driving. Many people look at these sports and see a man's world. Female athletes look at these sports and see a challenge. These women have broken the gender barrier to earn their place in history. Game on!

NAME: Eri Yoshida

SPORT: BASEBALL

BIRTHDAY: January 17, 1992

CRED: first female drafted by a professional Japanese baseball team

TRIVIA: Yoshida is one of the few players to throw a knuckleball pitch. With a knuckleball, the ball spins little, causing it to zig, zag, or spiral its way to the plate.

NAME: Julie Krone

SPORT: HORSE RACING

BIRTHDAY: July 24, 1963

CRED: first female jockey to win a Triple Crown race

TRIVIA: When Krone was a child, she was in gymnastics and almost joined the circus.

"I approached the sport like there wasn't a gender issue, and I wouldn't participate in the mind-set of 'she is just a girl.'"

NAME: Janet Guthrie

SPORT: AUTO RACING

BIRTHDAY: March 7, 1938

CRED: first woman to compete in the Indianapolis 500 and the Daytona 500

TRIVIA: Guthrie is an engineer who made it through the first round of cuts to be an astronaut.

NAME: Peggy Llewellyn

SPORT: PROSTOCK MOTORCYCLE RACING

BIRTHDAY: December 26, 1972

CRED: first woman of color to win a professional motorsports event

TRIVIA: Llewellyn is active in the Women's Sports Foundation's Go Girl Go! program, which encourages girls to exercise and be healthy.

NAME: Vonetta Flowers

SPORT: BOBSLEDDING

BIRTHDAY: October 29, 1973

CRED: first black athlete from any country to win a gold medal in the Winter Olympics

TRIVIA: Before bobsledding, Flowers hoped to compete in the Olympics as a long jumper. She failed to qualify. But then her husband saw a flyer asking track athletes to try out bobsledding. The rest is history.

ELISSA STEAMER

JULY 31, 1975–

When she began skateboarding, 10-year-old Elissa Steamer had never seen a girl on a board. Skateboarding was a boy's sport. But Steamer did it anyway. "I liked, you know, all things different. Saw somebody doing it. It was the '80s, and skating was big ... My dad was stoked on it. He'd buy me a skateboard for my birthday in July, and then he'd buy me a skateboard for Christmas."

In 1998 she won the first women's skateboarding competition at a World Cup skating event. Since then, she's won four X Games gold medals. And she was the first female skater in the Tony Hawk video games. She is one of the best female street skaters in the world. And she's an inspiration to skaters everywhere.

"SHE REALLY SET THE PACE FOR ALL GIRL SKATERS OUT THERE ... AND SORT OF MADE IT ACCEPTABLE AND POSSIBLE FOR A GIRL TO MAKE IT IN PROFESSIONAL SKATEBOARDING. BEFORE HER GIRLS DIDN'T HAVE ANYBODY TO LOOK UP TO, TO GO 'HEY, I COULD DO THAT TOO,' YOU KNOW. SO SHE REALLY PAVED THE WAY FOR SKATEBOARDING AND GIRLS."

—CHAD MUSKA, PRO SKATER

FAMOUS NAMES, FAMOUS FIGHT

The arena was full of waiting fans. I was there with a press pass on. Good thing I got that for free. No way I could have paid the 300 bucks for a ringside seat. This boxing match was going to be something special. Ali versus Frazier.

I better step back here. See, Muhammad Ali and Joe Frazier were big rivals in the 1970s.

They had three huge fights that drew huge crowds. But the fight I was at wasn't one of those. I was sitting in the arena in Verona, New York, watching their daughters box. And let me tell you, their rivalry was just as big as their dads'.

I was there to write a story for a small-town newspaper. Here's what I wrote.

LAILA ALI AND JACQUI FRAZIER DUKE IT OUT

Verona, NY—Thousands of fans gathered for the Ali-Frazier boxing match on June 8, 2001. Laila Ali and Jacqui Frazier duked it out, carrying on the rivalry their fathers started. Frazier out-punched Ali in the first rounds, but Ali seemed to gain strength as the match went on. Ali won the match by the decision of the judges.

Laila Ali has built an impressive boxing career. She has big shoes to fill, but she has a powerful jab to back it up. She was undefeated going into the match against Frazier.

Jacqui Frazier came to the match with her own undefeated record. She has not been tested as much as Ali. However, she shows a talent for combining hooks and jabs to knock her opponents out.

Their family names and pre-fight talk drew thousands of fans on TV and in the arena. While Ali came away with the win, both proved that female boxers can draw an audience. They also showed their worth as boxers and brought thousands of new fans to the sport of women's boxing.

LAILA ALI
DECEMBER 30, 1977–

JACQUI FRAZIER
DECEMBER 2, 1961–

MARGARET COURT

JULY 16, 1942-

In the 1960s, the biggest name on the tennis court was Australian Margaret Court. She burst onto the scene with a powerhouse serve that whizzed past her opponents. She would often return the ball before it hit the ground in a volley that was the strongest in women's tennis. Court is thought by many to be the greatest female tennis player of all time, and she has the stats to prove it.

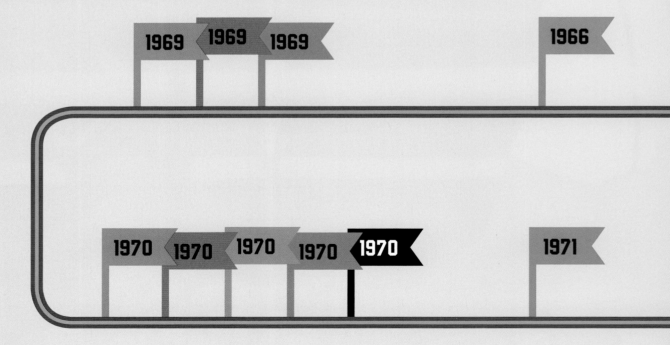

1960

1969 1969 1969 1966

1970 1970 1970 1970 1970 1971

⚑	AUSTRALIAN OPEN SINGLES TITLES
⚑	FRENCH OPEN SINGLES TITLES
⚑	WIMBLEDON SINGLES TITLES
⚑	U.S. OPEN SINGLES TITLES
⚑	**GRAND SLAM** (INCLUDES AUSTRALIAN OPEN, FRENCH OPEN, WIMBLEDON, AND U.S. OPEN)

1961   1962   1962   1962   1963   1963

1965   1965   1965   1964   1964

1973   1973   1973

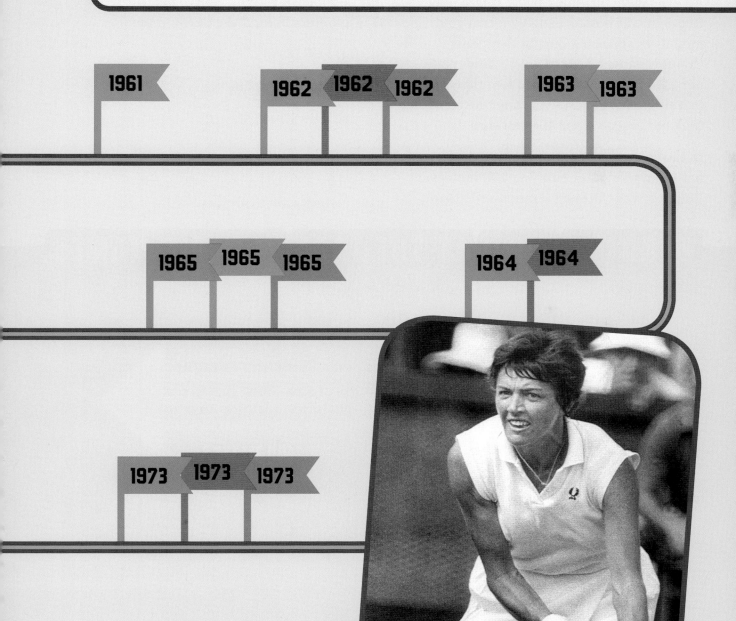

WILMA RUDOLPH

JUNE 23, 1940–NOVEMBER 12, 1994

All eyes were on young track star Wilma Rudolph. She had already won two gold medals in sprinting during the 1960 Olympic games. A third gold would make her the only woman ever to win three golds in a single Olympics. Everyone tensed as she took her place for the 100-m relay.

In the relay, each runner hands a baton to her teammate after running 100 meters. Rudolph was the last runner on the team.

By the time the baton came to her, the team was 2 meters behind the German team.

COULD SHE DO IT?

Rudolph took off sprinting.

Her muscles strained.

Sweat beaded her brow.

She pushed past the competition and carried her team to victory.

WINNING GOLD AT THE 1960 OLYMPIC GAMES

100-METER DASH

0 METERS

Finished in 11.0 seconds

100 METERS

200-METER DASH

0 METERS

RUDOLPH OUT FRONT AFTER THE BATON HAND-OFF DURING THE 100-METER RELAY.

The 1960 Olympics wasn't the first time Rudolph came from behind to win. As a child, Rudolph had polio that left her with a paralyzed leg. Her family took turns massaging the leg every night.

Each week she went to physical therapy to regain her strength. Doctors said she would never walk again.

She didn't walk ... she ran.

Finished in 24.0 seconds

RUDOLPH'S RECORD-SETTING THREE GOLD MEDALS ROCKETED HER TO SUPERSTARDOM. HER FAME ROSE ALMOST AS QUICKLY AS SHE RAN IN THOSE RACES.

FEARLESS FEMALES

Being an athlete takes strength and stamina. Being a champion takes courage. These women were tested by unbelievable obstacles. They overcame with a fearlessness that carried them to the top of their sports.

Surfer

BETHANY HAMILTON

FEBRUARY 8, 1990–

Hamilton lost her arm after a shark attack when she was 13 years old.

Before her several surgeries were even through, she was asking to go back in the water. Learning to surf again wasn't easy. She worked to adjust her balance and hand placement. She also started on a larger board and worked her way down to the smaller boards she had been used to. Within months of the attack, she was training again for competition.

Just two years after the attack, Hamilton took first place in her division in the National Scholastic Surfing Association National Championships.

Wheelchair Racer

JEAN DRISCOLL

NOVEMBER 18, 1966–

Driscoll was born with spina bifida, a disorder in which the spine is not fully formed.

Driscoll won her division in the Boston Marathon eight times. She is the only athlete in the history of the race to win eight times in any division. She has also earned 12 Paralympic medals, four of them gold.

Motocross Racer

ASHLEY FIOLEK

OCTOBER 22, 1990–

Fiolek has been deaf since birth. She uses the vibrations of her bike to tell her when to shift gears.

Fiolek is a two-time X Games gold medalist and one of the biggest names in motocross.

Skier

LAUREN WOOLSTENCROFT

NOVEMBER 24, 1981–

Woolstencroft was born without her left arm below the elbow and without both legs below the knee.

Woolstencroft won a total of 10 Olympic medals in her career, including five gold medals at the 2010 Winter Paralympics. She is one of the most celebrated Paralympians in history.

Track and Field

AIMEE MULLINS

1976–

Mullins was born missing bones in both legs. Doctors amputated both legs below the knee.

Mullins has set world records for the long jump, 100-m sprint, and 200-m sprint.

Representative Mink

Representative Green

Patsy Mink and Edith Green

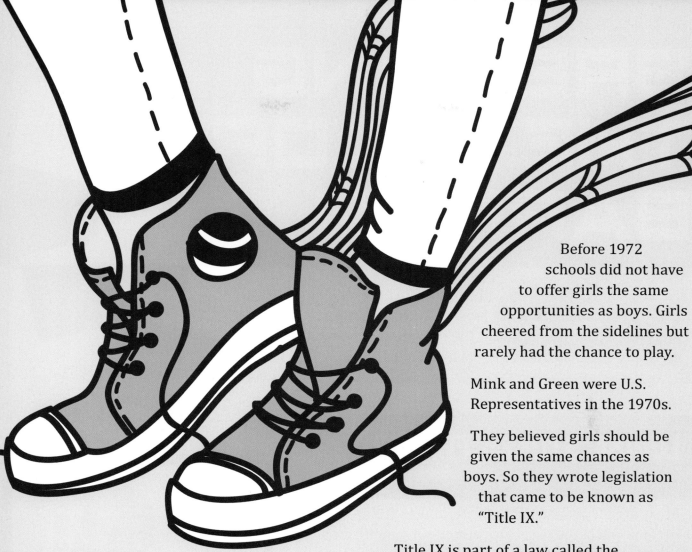

Before 1972 schools did not have to offer girls the same opportunities as boys. Girls cheered from the sidelines but rarely had the chance to play.

Mink and Green were U.S. Representatives in the 1970s.

They believed girls should be given the same chances as boys. So they wrote legislation that came to be known as "Title IX."

Title IX is part of a law called the Education Amendments of 1972. It stated that no school could discriminate against women, including in sports. Not everyone was in favor of Title IX. But despite the disagreement, Title IX passed in both the House of Representatives and the Senate. The Education Amendments were signed into law on June 23, 1972.

Patsy Mink and Edith Green never broke sports records or won championships. But they did make a huge change in sports.

In fact without them, schools might not have girls sports today.

Title IX only addresses equality in schools. Female athletes still fight to be recognized in their sports. Ski jumper Alissa Johnson worked to make women's ski jumping an Olympic sport. Skier Sarah Burke worked to have female superpipe skiing events included in the Winter Olympics.

BREAKING THE COLOR BARRIER

For years African-American athletes had to fight for their right to compete. Black females fought bravely and endured terrible injustice. Their work—and their sacrifices—opened doors for female athletes today.

LOUISE STOKES FRASER

1913-1978

As a gifted track and field athlete, Louise Stokes Fraser became one of the first black athletes to qualify for a U.S. Olympic team. But success did not come easily for black athletes in the 1930s. At the time African-Americans were treated poorly and discriminated against.

Fraser's experience was no different. She earned a spot on the 1932 and 1936 Olympic track and field teams. She traveled with the teams to the events. But both times, she was surprised to discover that she had been replaced by a white athlete. She was forced to sit in the stands, watching someone else compete in her place.

Fraser did not let her disappointments at the Olympics keep her from sports. She went on to become a professional bowler. She also founded the Colored Women's Bowling League in 1941. Today Fraser is remembered for paving the way for future generations of black athletes.

ALTHEA GIBSON

AUGUST 25, 1927–SEPTEMBER 28, 2003

Althea Gibson was born to hold a tennis racket. But in the 1940s African-American athletes were segregated from white athletes. They weren't allowed to play in major championships.

Althea played in tournaments for black players, winning 10 straight championships. She even went to Florida A&M on a sports scholarship. But after college, the tennis doors were closed. Althea almost quit playing.

Finally in 1951 Althea was invited to play at Wimbledon, becoming the first African-American to play that event. She went on to win five Grand Slam titles, win at Wimbledon and the U.S. Open, and break the color barrier for future black players.

DOMINIQUE DAWES

NOVEMBER 20, 1976–

When Dominique Dawes began to show promise as an athlete, there were few black gymnasts. That didn't stop her from setting her sights high. By age 11, she dedicated herself to the sport, waking up at 5 each morning to practice before school. Rather than focusing on one event, Dawes showed promise in them all—balance beam, uneven bars, vault, and floor exercises. She won national championships and silver medals at the 1993 and 1994 World Championships.

Dawes made history at the 1996 Olympics, when she became the first African-American woman to earn a gold medal in gymnastics. She performed solid routines in each event, leading the team of seven gymnasts to gold.

OLGA KORBUT

MAY 16, 1955–

I WAS THERE AT THE 1972 OLYMPICS IN MUNICH, GERMANY. I WAS A SPECTATOR IN THE STANDS DURING THE GYMNASTICS COMPETITION. I WAS SO EXCITED TO SEE THE BEST OF THE BEST COMPETING ON A WORLD STAGE. WHAT I ENDED UP WATCHING, THOUGH, WAS HISTORY BEING MADE.

Tiny Olga Korbut stole the show. She was a 17-year-old girl from the Soviet Union. She was so small, I thought a big breeze might blow her away. But just because she was small, doesn't mean she wasn't strong. Oh boy, was she strong. That girl stunned us all.

During that competition, Olga did a backflip off the top of the uneven bars and swung her body around the lower bar. Then she flew backward to grab the top bar again. It was really a death-defying feat. In fact, the move was later banned because it's so dangerous.

She was a daredevil. She landed a backflip on the balance beam at the Olympics too. No one had ever done that before. She really was something to watch. And it wasn't just me who thought so. The whole world had Olga fever. Kids all over the world joined gymnastics clubs to be like her. Her crazy acrobatic moves changed gymnastics forever.

BONNIE BLAIR

MARCH 18, 1964–

IMAGINE A CAR DRIVING 25 MILES (40 KM) PER HOUR.

NOW IMAGINE GOING THAT SPEED ON ICE SKATES.

THAT IS THE SPORT OF SPEED SKATING.

For many fans speed skating is defined by one of its most famous faces—Bonnie Blair. Before the 1994 Olympics, Blair had won three Olympic gold medals. But at the '94 Olympics, she made history. She sped to victory in the 500, tying the record for most gold medals. But she had one more race. If she could win, she would be the first American woman to win five gold medals. It wouldn't be easy.

Blair was up against a fierce competitor from China. The starting gun went off, and both skaters started strong. After the first lap, Blair was behind. But she gave it everything she had in the second lap. Fans cheered wildly from the stands. Blair pulled ahead. She finished the race a full 1.38 seconds ahead of her competitor. As the famous face of speed skating, she brought new fans to the sport and is forever a speed skating legend.

NATALIE COUGHLIN

BIO CARD

Born: August 23, 1982
Sport: swimming

- first American woman to win six medals in a single Olympics
- earned 12 Olympic medals in her career, more than any other U.S. woman in history

	Gold	Silver	Bronze
Athens, 2004	2	2	1
Beijing, 2008	1	2	3
London, 2012	0	0	1

JENNIE FINCH

BIO CARD

Born: September 3, 1980
Sport: softball

With a controlled, fast pitch, she struck out more than 1,000 batters in her college career at the University of Arizona.

With Team USA Finch won two World Championships and Olympic gold.

	Gold	Silver	Bronze
Athens, 2004	1	0	0
Beijing, 2008	0	0	0

Many women have won Olympic gold, pushing harder and faster than their competitors. These athletes have more than just skill. They have personality and power that make their gold shine a little brighter.

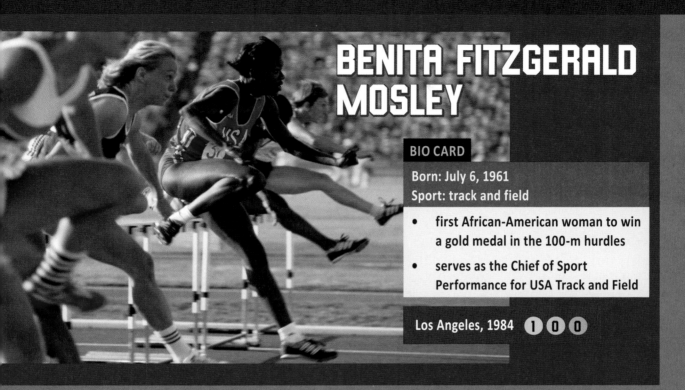

BENITA FITZGERALD MOSLEY

BIO CARD

Born: July 6, 1961
Sport: track and field

- first African-American woman to win a gold medal in the 100-m hurdles
- serves as the Chief of Sport Performance for USA Track and Field

Los Angeles, 1984 **1 0 0**

LINDSEY VONN

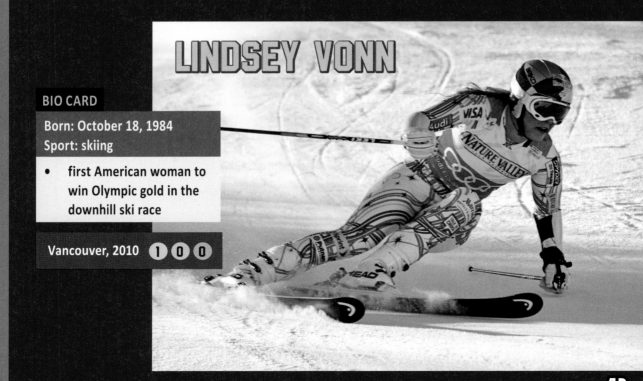

BIO CARD

Born: October 18, 1984
Sport: skiing

- first American woman to win Olympic gold in the downhill ski race

Vancouver, 2010 **1 0 0**

TRACY CAULKINS

JANUARY 11, 1963–

She may not be a household name, but to those who know the sport of swimming, she's a legend. Tracy Caulkins seemed to be built for swimming. She was able to bend her knees backward, kicking dolphinlike through the water. Unlike other swimmers, she wasn't best in one or two strokes. She dominated everything—the breaststroke, butterfly, freestyle, and backstroke.

She is considered one of the best female swimmers of all time.

Caulkins is the only swimmer to set American records for all four strokes. At the 1984 Olympics, she won three gold medals. By the end of her career, she had set 63 American records. Her 48 national titles is the most won by any U.S. swimmer in history—male or female.

BREASTSTROKE: In the breaststroke, a swimmer's arms move out from the chest, much like a frog swims. The swimmer faces forward and does not rotate side to side.

FREESTYLE: In the freestyle stroke, the arms move in a crawling motion while the feet kick.

BUTTERFLY: In this stroke, a swimmer's outstretched arms move in circles, while the feet kick like a dolphin's fin.

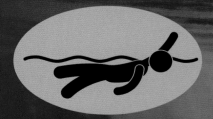

BACKSTROKE: Just like it sounds, the backstroke is swum on a swimmer's back, with the arms reaching ahead and the feet kicking behind.

PERFECT 10

NADIA COMANECI

NOVEMBER 12, 1961–

There was no "perfect" in gymnastics. Gymnasts competed for points on a scale of 1-10. But no one had ever gotten a 10 ... until the 1976 Olympics.

When Nadia Comaneci from Romania performed on the uneven bars, she soared between the top and bottom bars. She did two handstands and spun around.

She dismounted in a perfect swan dive without the slightest hop. It was simply a flawless performance.

After the routine everyone watched the scoreboard. What would the score be? Finally, it appeared. The scoreboard flashed a "1.00." The board did not have enough digits to show the true score. Comaneci had earned **a perfect 10.**

MARY LOU RETTON

JANUARY 24, 1968–

Growing up in a small town in West Virginia, Mary Lou Retton had few opportunities to play sports. There was one dance studio in her town, but Retton knew that dance was not for her.

Kelly Clark

JULY 26, 1983–

In her third and final run at the 2012 Winter X Games, snowboarder Kelly Clark had a perfect 10 of a different kind. She slid to her starting position on the massive SuperPipe, singing to the music blasting from her headphones. Then, she was off—gliding up and down the sides of the pipe with unbelievable air time. She twisted and turned her board as she seemed to fly above the pipe. The crowd and TV announcers cheered when she delivered a perfect 1080. Also called a 10, the move includes three complete turns in the air. She is the first woman to ever land a 1080 in competition. Clark's aggressive style is now the gold standard in competitive snowboarding.

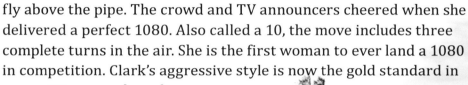

"Then came the summer of 1976, and I was 7 years old, and I was glued to the television set watching my first Olympic games ... and I watched a little girl named Nadia from Romania do all these incredible things with her body."

"That's it," Retton decided, "that's what I want to do." She grew to love the sport of gymnastics. She trained with famous coach

Retton made it to the Olympics in the summer of 1984. Her last individual of the games was the vault. She soare the apparatus, twisting through the She landed perfectly, without taking slightest step on the mat. The crowd chanted, "10, 10, 10!"

And the scoreboard answered with R perfect 10.

FLORENCE GRIFFITH-JOYNER

DECEMBER 21, 1959–SEPTEMBER 21, 1998

She was competing in the 100-m final, a sprint that lasts just seconds. She lined up on the starting blocks with her famous long, painted nails. At the starting gun, she was off. For half of the dash, she was running alongside the other runners. But it's the second half where "Flo Jo" built her reputation.

It was the 1988 Olympics, and Florence Griffith-Joyner had just shown the world what she could do. She finished far ahead of the other runners, setting the Olympic record for the 100-m dash in just 10.54 seconds. It was not a world record—Flo Jo had set that record during the Olympic Trials at 10.49 seconds.

That world record—and one for the 200-m run—still stands, despite being set decades ago.

Griffith-Joyner is still called the fastest woman in the world. She earned three gold medals in track and field and two silver medals. She changed the sport of track and field by setting the bar so high, no one has yet to reach it.

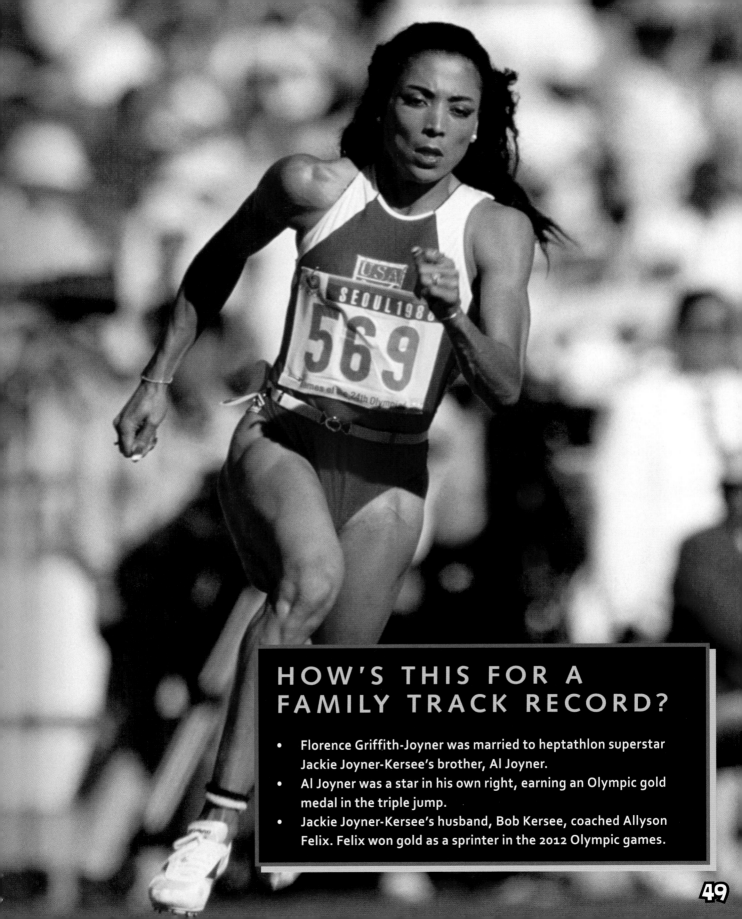

HOW'S THIS FOR A FAMILY TRACK RECORD?

- Florence Griffith-Joyner was married to heptathlon superstar Jackie Joyner-Kersee's brother, Al Joyner.
- Al Joyner was a star in his own right, earning an Olympic gold medal in the triple jump.
- Jackie Joyner-Kersee's husband, Bob Kersee, coached Allyson Felix. Felix won gold as a sprinter in the 2012 Olympic games.

PERFECT

Some things in life are just better together.
- peanut butter and jelly   • socks and shoes
- Kerri Walsh-Jennings and Misty May-Traenor

MISTY MAY-TRAENOR

0 0

JULY 30, 1977–

- played in her first volleyball tournament at age 8 with her father, who played volleyball in the 1968 Olympics

- as team captain at Long Beach State University, led her team to become the first women's NCAA volleyball team to go undefeated

- placed 5th in the 2000 Olympics with partner Holly McPeak

LET'S GET TOGETHER

In the 1990s Walsh-Jennings and May-Traenor played against each other in college. Walsh-Jennings saw how amazing May-Traenor was as a player and looked up to her. At one tournament, Walsh-Jennings even asked May-Traenor for her autograph. But it wasn't until the 2000 Olympics that they even thought about teaming up in beach volleyball. Walsh-Jennings' and May-Traenor's families bumped into each other at that Olympics.

They began talking about what a great team the women would make. In 2001 they played their first game together. Their amazing skills and dedication made them a terrific team. But it was their deep friendship that made them so powerful.

After winning their third Olympic gold, May-Traenor said, "The first two medals, I think was more volleyball. The friendship we had was there, but it was all volleyball, volleyball. This was so much more about the friendship, the togetherness, the journey. And volleyball was just a small part of it."

PAIRING

Individually Walsh-Jennings and May-Traenor are stellar volleyball players. But together, they are considered the greatest beach volleyball team in history.

00 KERRI WALSH-JENNINGS

AUGUST 30, 1978–

- named First-Team All-American in all four seasons that she played at Stanford University

- played indoor volleyball at the 2000 Olympics, finishing fourth with her team

- named the Association of Volleyball Players' Best Offensive Player and MVP in 2003 and 2004

DYNAMIC DUO

WON 112 CONSECUTIVE MATCHES IN 2008

EARNED GOLD MEDALS IN THE 2004, 2008, AND 2012 OLYMPICS, LOSING JUST ONE OF 43 SETS

NAMED FEDERATION INTERNATIONALE DE VOLLEYBALL TOUR CHAMPIONS IN 2002

NAMED TEAM OF THE YEAR IN 2003

MIA HAMM

MARCH 17, 1972–

 Started playing soccer when she was 5 years old.

 Olympic champion, leading her team to gold medals at the 1996 and 2004 Games

 Considered the best female soccer player in history, playing for 17 years with the U.S. national soccer team.

 Collected a multitude of awards, including USA's Female Athlete of the Year five years in a row, MVP of the Women's Cup, and three ESPY awards, including Soccer Player of the Year and Female Athlete of the Year

 Early in her career, she had great success. At 15 years old, Hamm became the youngest person to play for a U.S. national soccer team. And at 19 years old, she was the youngest player ever to appear at a World Cup.

 Record-breaking player, who has scored more international goals than any other player, male or female

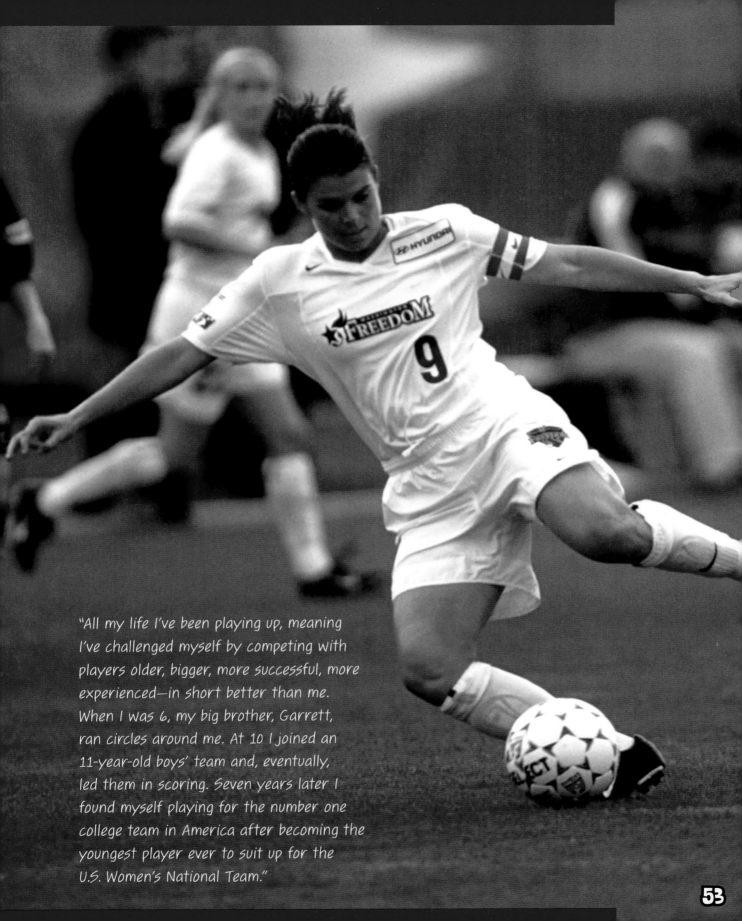

"All my life I've been playing up, meaning I've challenged myself by competing with players older, bigger, more successful, more experienced—in short better than me. When I was 6, my big brother, Garrett, ran circles around me. At 10 I joined an 11-year-old boys' team and, eventually, led them in scoring. Seven years later I found myself playing for the number one college team in America after becoming the youngest player ever to suit up for the U.S. Women's National Team."

SISTERS AND STARS

Serena Williams

Born: September 26, 1981

Greatest Win: 1999 U.S. Open; Serena became the first African-American to win a singles championship since 1958.

Strength: power plus speed

Struggle: had several health issues in 2011 including a blood clot in her lung; suffered an ankle injury in 2012

Venus Williams

Born: June 17, 1980

Greatest Win: 2007 Wimbledon; Venus became one of only four women in history to win the event four times.

Strength: powerful serve

Struggle: suffers from Sjogren's syndrome, a disorder causing fatigue and sore joints

Venus and Serena Williams exploded onto the tennis scene in the 1990s. They were like nothing women's tennis had seen before. They were stronger and more talented than the average women's tennis players. Both had powerful serves and strokes, built over decades of training. They began winning tournaments at age 10. By 1999 they were ranked as two of the top five tennis players in the world.

Both Venus and Serena have won an impressive number of singles championship titles—43 each. Playing powerfully as a team, they have won dozens of doubles titles. Their skills and star power have drawn new fans to women's tennis and brought a new level of competition to the game.

Daring Dancers

Anna Pavlova

FEBRUARY 12, 1881–JANUARY 23, 1931

When she was young, Anna Pavlova was mocked for being too thin. But her thin limbs were strong, and her grace was unmatched. She became the world's most famous ballerina. Audiences were awed by the physical feat of her most famous performance, *The Dying Swan*. It was three minutes long, but moving enough to be one of the most famous pieces ever performed. Pavlova performed the piece herself more than 4,000 times. She was a traditional ballerina whose dainty style remains the standard for classical ballet.

Isadora Duncan

MAY 27, 1877–SEPTEMBER 14, 1927

Isadora Duncan had little patience for classical ballet. She did not dance in slippers or a tutu. Instead, she wowed audiences of the early 20th century in bare feet and a tunic. Duncan's style was natural and flowing, nothing the world of dance had ever seen before. Her unique style is now called modern dance, and she is considered the mother of the modern dance movement.

Martha Graham

MAY 11, 1894–APRIL 1, 1991

Martha Graham was not interested in being beautiful or looking graceful. She wanted to dance with real emotion, to tell a story with movement. In 1935 she did just that with *Frontier*. Graham created and performed the seven-minute dance about a pioneer woman. In the process, she pioneered a new age of dance.

Are dancers athletes? For many people dance is not the first word to come to mind when they think of athletics. Throughout the history of dance, dancers have struggled to prove themselves as athletes. As the popularity of dance grows every year, and with the growth of athletic styles such as hip-hop, dancers are finally getting the recognition they deserve.

Sofia Boutella danced in a Nike campaign that promotes the dancer as an athlete. Alicia Graf Mack is another popular dancer who sees herself as an athlete. "Dancing requires us to train every day," she explains, "to build a certain type of muscle memory ... in that sense, I do consider myself an athlete."

MICHELLE WIE

OCTOBER 11, 1989–

Michelle Wie is one of the most famous female golfers. She has finished in the top 10 in seven major championships, and she's just out of college. For a record like that, she had to start young.

age 4 – begins golfing

age 10 – qualifies for the USGA Women's Amateur Public Links Championship

age 13 – becomes the youngest player ever to qualify for the Ladies Professional Golf Association (LPGA) tour

age 15 – becomes the first female golfer to qualify for a men's tournament

age 19 – wins the Lorena Ochoa Invitational

age 20 – wins the Canadian Women's Open

Annika Sorenstam

OCTOBER 9, 1970-

The crowds were larger than usual for the PGA tour event in Fort Worth, Texas, on May 23, 2003. The reason? There was a woman playing. Annika Sorenstam was the first woman to play in a PGA tour since Babe Didrikson Zaharias in 1945. Some said she had no place in a men's tour. Others said they wouldn't play alongside her. But Sorenstam just focused on her game. She didn't make the cut into the second round, but she had accomplished something far greater.

"I came here to test myself. I'm proud of the way I was focusing and proud of the decisions I made and that I stuck to them. And that's why I am here. I wanted to see if I could do it."

Sorenstam won 89 tournaments around the world and is considered by many to be the best golfer in the LPGA. She became the first female to earn more than $20 million. Thanks to Sorenstam's star power, women's golf is more popular than ever before.

IN GOLF A TOUR IS A SERIES OF PROFESSIONAL TOURNAMENTS, OFTEN GROUPED BY WHERE THEY TAKE PLACE. KATHY WHITWORTH HOLDS THE RECORD FOR THE NUMBER OF U.S. TOUR WINS WITH 88. THAT RECORD BEATS ANY MALE OR FEMALE GOLFER IN TOUR HISTORY.

Soaring

Peggy Fleming

JULY 27, 1948–

Peggy Fleming began skating at just 9 years old. She won her first competition two years later and decided that competitive skating was the life for her. She dreamed of joining the U.S. national figure skating team and began training to do just that. She worked with coach Bill Kipp. In addition to training Fleming, Kipp coached skaters on the U.S. figure skating team. But tragedy struck in 1961. Kipp and all 18 members of the U.S. team were killed in a plane crash on their way to the World Championships.

Fleming was devastated by the loss of her coach and fellow skaters. The U.S. figure skating program was devastated too. Under a new coach, Fleming showed the world that the U.S. skating program was still alive. She won the world championships in 1966, 1967, and 1968.

When Fleming glided onto the ice at the 1968 Olympics, the pressure was on. She skated a routine with amazingly fluid movements. Fleming won the only gold the United States would take at the Games that winter.

Katarina Witt

DECEMBER 3, 1965–

Katarina Witt went into the 1988 Olympics ready to defend the gold medal she won four years earlier. She had chosen to skate her long program to the opera *Carmen*. Her rival, Debi Thomas, came ready to unseat Witt. Her chosen music? *Carmen*. The media hyped the Battle of the *Carmens*, but Witt stayed focused.

The strongest part of Witt's skating had always been style and movement to the music—she told a story on the ice. According to the judges, she told the story of Carmen better than her rival. She took the gold medal and helped show a generation of young skaters that grace and elegance are just as important as technical jumps.

on Ice

Dorothy Hamill

AUGUST 26, 1956–

With swift spinning and flying leaps, Hamill won the U.S. Championships in 1974, 1975, and 1976. Her routines included the unique "Hamill Camel," which she invented. The move began with a standing spin and evolved to a sitting spin with amazing speed.

Hamill made it to the 1976 Olympics, but many doubted she could win the gold. She was often nervous before skating and was very shy in front of a crowd. She sometimes left the ice in tears before skating. Could she keep her cool under the pressure of the Olympics?

If she felt the pressure as she skated onto the ice for her long program, there was no way to tell. She skated a nearly flawless routine with graceful spirals and her signature spins. But it was her sweet face, bobbed hair, and willpower that turned her into a household name. She won the gold medal, that time saving the tears for the winner's podium.

Michelle Kwan

JULY 7, 1980–

Michelle Kwan is one of the best known names in figure skating. Her daring moves made her a fan favorite and a fierce competitor. She skated daring routines, landing seven triple jumps in one program. A triple jump requires three complete turns in the air.

Over her career, Kwan won more Olympic medals and championships than any other U.S. figure skater in history. She never won an Olympic gold, but her golden personality and talent more than made up for it.

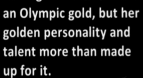

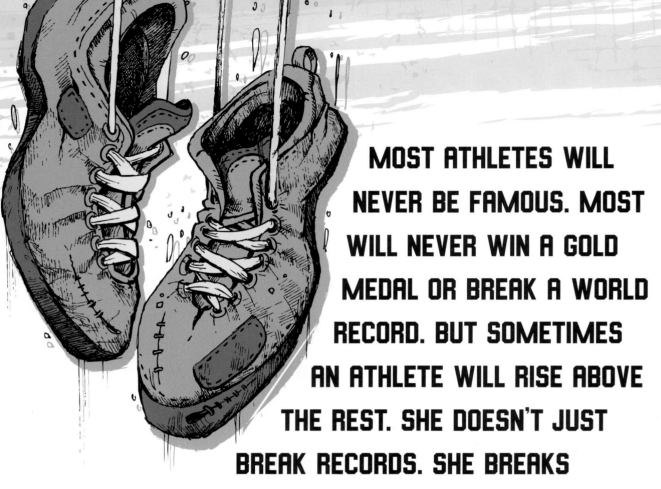

MOST ATHLETES WILL NEVER BE FAMOUS. MOST WILL NEVER WIN A GOLD MEDAL OR BREAK A WORLD RECORD. BUT SOMETIMES AN ATHLETE WILL RISE ABOVE THE REST. SHE DOESN'T JUST BREAK RECORDS. SHE BREAKS BARRIERS AND INFLUENCES GENERATIONS OF ATHLETES TO COME.

HER POWER, STRENGTH, AND SPIRIT CHANGES SPORTS FOREVER. AND SHE PROVES THAT PLAYING LIKE A GIRL ROCKS!

"EACH OF US HAS A FIRE IN OUR HEARTS FOR SOMETHING.
IT'S OUR GOAL IN LIFE TO FIND IT AND KEEP IT LIT."
- MARY LOU RETTON

MANY OF THESE WOMEN WON AND LOST OVER SEVERAL DECADES.
THEIR PLACEMENT ON THE TIMELINE REFLECTS THE DECADE IN WHICH
THEY TRULY MADE HISTORY.

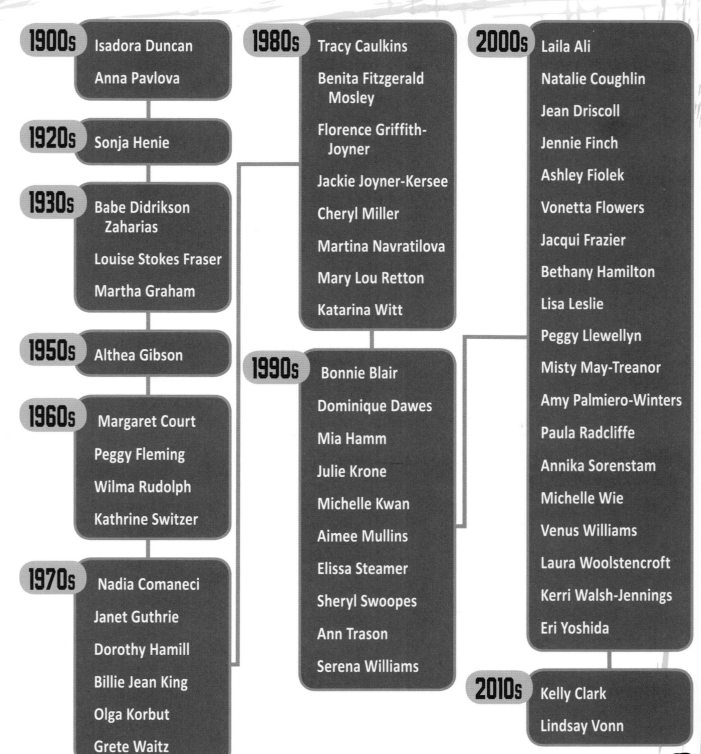

1900s
Isadora Duncan
Anna Pavlova

1920s
Sonja Henie

1930s
Babe Didrikson Zaharias
Louise Stokes Fraser
Martha Graham

1950s
Althea Gibson

1960s
Margaret Court
Peggy Fleming
Wilma Rudolph
Kathrine Switzer

1970s
Nadia Comaneci
Janet Guthrie
Dorothy Hamill
Billie Jean King
Olga Korbut
Grete Waitz

1980s
Tracy Caulkins
Benita Fitzgerald Mosley
Florence Griffith-Joyner
Jackie Joyner-Kersee
Cheryl Miller
Martina Navratilova
Mary Lou Retton
Katarina Witt

1990s
Bonnie Blair
Dominique Dawes
Mia Hamm
Julie Krone
Michelle Kwan
Aimee Mullins
Elissa Steamer
Sheryl Swoopes
Ann Trason
Serena Williams

2000s
Laila Ali
Natalie Coughlin
Jean Driscoll
Jennie Finch
Ashley Fiolek
Vonetta Flowers
Jacqui Frazier
Bethany Hamilton
Lisa Leslie
Peggy Llewellyn
Misty May-Treanor
Amy Palmiero-Winters
Paula Radcliffe
Annika Sorenstam
Michelle Wie
Venus Williams
Laura Woolstencroft
Kerri Walsh-Jennings
Eri Yoshida

2010s
Kelly Clark
Lindsay Vonn

INDEX

READ MORE

Bryant, Jill. *Women Athletes Who Changed the World.* Great Women of Achievement. New York: Rosen Pub., 2012.

Stout, Glenn. *Yes She Can! Women's Sports Pioneers.* Good Sports. Boston: Houghton Mifflin Harcourt, 2011.

Tougas, Shelley. *Girls Rule! Amazing Tales of Female Leaders.* Girls Rock. North Mankato, Minn.: Capstone Press, 2014.

INTERNET SITES

FactHound offers a safe, fun way to find Internet sites related to this book. All of the sites on FactHound have been researched by our staff.

Here's all you do:

Visit *www.facthound.com*

Type in this code:
9781476502335